Journeys Become Stories

poetic experiments
Chris Gibson

Contents

Negative Space
A Day in the Wilderness
The Train and the City
The Night Shift
White Noise
News
Climbing Trees
The Venetian Canal
The Gift
Little Aspirations
Recognition
The Tin Can
Lindsay Kemp
Lines of London
By the Sea
The Flame
Serene Tableau
One Step at a Time
The Cooling Towers
Cross-Pollination
Wisp of Imagination
Temporal Magic
The Fading Day
Latent Image
The Poem
Nature's Hand
Inspiration
Ugly
Head Over Heels
Métro, Boulot, Dodo
The Tower Block

Negative Space

The device strapped to my wrist
Tracks my steps, my sleep.
It could produce a book of charts;
The facts of my life told by the second.

An eager reader would find:
I walk about six kilometres a day,
I sleep eight hours.
Each day distilled.

My old life drawing teacher
Had a mantra:
To look for the 'negative space',
The space around objects.

There is so much negative space
Around that little gadget;
So much life not quantified,
Not shown on its tiny screen.

But could this small machine
Be the forefather of some,
Greater all-seeing thing?
That would know me better than I do?

A Day in the Wilderness

A day in the wilderness.
Our beautiful concrete world.
A place we have sculpted,
You and I.
To match our dreams.

The Train and the City

We spread ourselves at intervals
Down the platform.
We shuffle as new people enter.
We fit together simply.

One train replaces another,
It hurries us off neatly
Like some housekeeper of old;
Discreetly tidying up.

This city is a machine.
This line a conveyor.
And here we stand patiently
Waiting to be taken.

The Night Shift

A caffeine-induced night shift,
Completing spreadsheets in my sleep.
Each time I wake, I feel closer;
Some perfect formula within reach:
Happiness, the meaning of life?
An epic feat that will be forgotten
As I wake to morning light.

White Noise

The wind rattles window frames:
The house shaken by the elements.

We are closed in.
We are close.

Here we feel safe, together;
Cocooned.

These four walls are the world.
The white noise outside is a void.

News

A jumble of headlines.
Those beckoning voices.

I devour them:
Scraps of news and gossip.

They make a fine bed.
A hamster's nest.

Cocooning myself,
I imagine they are the world.

Climbing Trees

Do you remember those days?
It felt like we were climbing trees;
Our perspective changing by the branch;
Life's secrets revealed.

As we grew the climb continued.
And I wondered, looking back,
Why we still carried on,
Why we still pushed ever-forward?

Was it beauty we were chasing?
Or the promise of something new?
Either way it kept us young.
Our agile minds in constant flux.

The Venetian Canal

The Venetian canal,
Usually topaz green,
Looks magnolia in this light.

If you lived here you might miss it.
But to a stranger it is striking;
Beautiful, a subtle alchemy.

The Gift

Coffee in hand
(You and I know)
To sober up.

Ordinary life only
Palatable by
Brief exposure.

I'm submerged
In music;
It's a blanket.

The downpour
Of the morning
Turning to sun.

And this day,
Bit by bit,
May yet be bright.

Little Aspirations

True to type
The man with Poirot's moustache,
Alighted at Sloane Square.

I aspire too, to be
The man in Peter Jones
With the RAF haircut.

Or the elderly woman
Leaving the cafe
With sculpted hair and pearls.

Imagine waking up in a bed
Immaculate as snow
To a life as pure as linen.

Recognition

A teenager flipping pages
In a library.
Not reading;
Looking for recognition.

Waiting to hear a voice;
A key word;
A sign;
A shared experience.

She said:
"Lay a book on my chest"
He was caught by the sentiment,
He wanted to feel every word.

The Tin Can

The wind pushes.

The train carriage judders.

This tin can is more hardy than it seems.

A light rain decorates the window.

The elements are close today

As we slow into a station.

The scrub of trees at the platform

Seem greener, more forest-like

As they wave a slow-motion welcome.

Lindsay Kemp

A neat, neat world,
Papered with bright billboard images.
Tidy, friendly, very safe.

To live a life that cut like a knife.
A life of colour and feeling.
Burning and original.

We follow fashions:
Our subdued blues, greys, blacks.
And huddle close, self-contained.

Have we been burned?
Have we been scarred?
Could life be somehow, something more?

Lines of London

Following the lines of London
One Sunday morning
A different city emerges.

Silent streets expose
Broad brush strokes of history
Painted beneath the new.

Walking amongst heroes,
Amongst tyrants,
This place becomes a theatre.

And do we each
Wish ourselves up there?
Called forward to tread the boards.

By the Sea

Do you remember that night,
In the cottage by the sea?
The roar of the waves so close.
For me, an adventure.
For you, it brought fear.

I thought of Dorothy Gale,
(That little girl from Kansas)
Running from the winds.
As if the same power might propel us
To some enchanted land.

The Flame

The slate sky;
The flame of summer
Rudely extinguished.

Life returns
Crisp golds and browns
Turn green.

And what a summer!
The beautiful Janus-face
Of global warming.

Serene Tableau

A beautiful day starts like this:
Cool air, and fresh.
A pastel blue sky.

We, cut-out figures,
Ready to be placed
In some serene tableau.

One Step at a Time

Single-use plastic.
Palm oil.

The air miles
I have clocked up.

The energy burned
For an online search.

These confusing times
Are paralysing.

It is difficult
To walk the right path.

Maybe it is just enough
To take one step at a time.

Cooling Towers

All that power,
A marvel, of sorts.

The rush of water
Pounding.

We stand awed.
A human feat.

Looking up:
A concrete waterfall.

Cross Pollination

Hotdog with onions?
Is that candyfloss,
And sawdust?

My street
Smells like the Big Top!
A strange cross pollination.

Our senses fool us.
We're transported
By mere association.

Wisp of Imagination

A wisp of imagination,
Carried like a ribbon
Of cigarette smoke.

I want to turn my finger
In the air
And make a shape.

To transform
And give movement
To a fading thing.

And to create art
From nothing;
Beautiful as life.

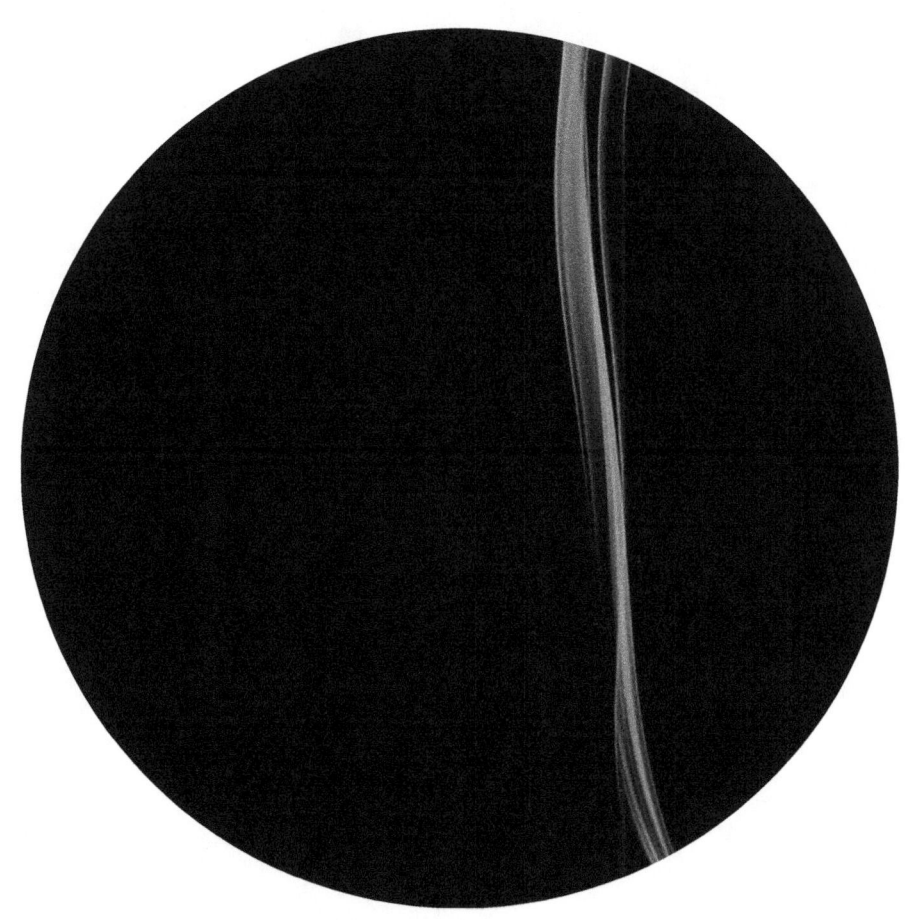

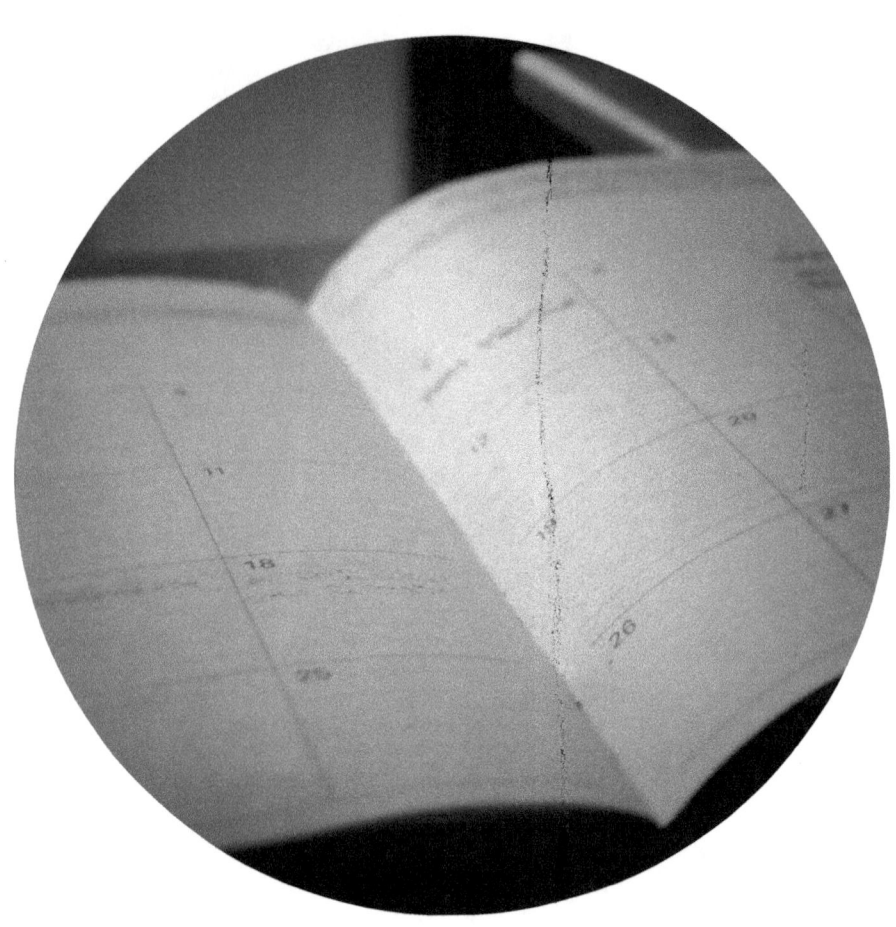

Temporal Magic

If life is just a concatenation of days
(Each new hour stitched to the last.)

How is it, we can inhabit the past?
And revisit moments long gone.

Sometimes it's a sound, a smell.
We're transported, the future put aside.

With it, our emotions reignited.
A temporal kind of magic.

The past tangles with the present.
Our life (a ball of wool) tumbles on.

The Fading Day

White sky, and the
Pale winter sun.
Flat green-yellow country
Rolls past the window.

We judder along
Wrapped blanket-like,
Soft as the mist
That clings to the hills.

Winter has been
Comforting and mild.
A gentler season than
Usual.

Time blurs on the road
Hours become minutes;
A day written-off. To be
Forgotten on arrival.

Latent Image

A man on the bonnet of a car.
In a ditch.
In Doncaster.

A strange sight
To start the day,
Through the window of the bus.

The man stretched out,
Reaching for something.
Supported by a friend.

The bus turns and
The moment passes.
I'm jolted back.

I pick up my book,
But can't read
For the vivid latent image.

The Poem

Poetry:
A still life,
An image.

Time slowed
Right down
To a stop.

A space opens
Between the writer
And the reader.

And momentarily
Two lives
Converge.

Nature's Hand

A blast of cold air.
Leaves under foot.
A new season upon us.

Do we change?
(Like Cathy and Heathcliff)
With the climate?

Do I become autumn,
As summer cools,
As I wrap up close?

Like Wilde's portrait of Dorian
My face is altered;
Pencilled in by nature's hand.

Inspiration

It comes and goes:
Inspiration.

Sometimes a crash.
Sometimes gentle, imperceptible.

The surfers are out today.
Lying on their boards.

Waiting for that gentle swell
To break.

At the sea wall, I look out.
And hold my breath in expectation.

Ugly

The landscape is ugly
This bitter winter's morning.

Trees of different shapes
Mesh muddily together.

Greens of the scrub
Blend into the dirt.

The shock off-white clouds
Make the horizon inky grey.

In the passing gardens:
A clothes airer, a broken swing.

The world is not its best
This early morning commute.

Head Over Heels

The relentless churn.
Beautiful products,
Pre-programmed to expire.

All these objects, these jewels
Seem to age in my grasping hands,
To fade beneath my wanting glare.

I want only the new
The glistening,
The perfect.

How might we breathe new life
Into the barely old?
And fall head over heels once more?

Métro, Boulot, Dodo

Gravel under foot;
I trudge to the station.
Days often so similar.

The Situationists
Mapped our days:
Métro, boulot, dodo.

They showed us repetition.
Routines plotted on a map.
Day after day for a year.

How would my map look?
A thick line for my commute.
Spidery lines of other trips.

For a each of us a pattern.
Each unique in its way.
Detailed as a fingerprint.

The Tower Block

Lives stacked together.
One opinion against another.

Behind the gleaming glass,
A patchwork of lifestyles.

We pass by on the train
And glance in;

To inhabit, for a moment
Another person's dream.

Image Credits

Negative Space - Chris Gibson
White Noise - Valentin Muller
News - Thomas Charters
The Gift - Reza Shayestehpour
Little Aspirations - Craig Whitehead
Lindsay Kemp - Alison Donovan Rouse
Lines of London - Max Busse
Serene Tableau - Lex Sirikiat
One Step at a Time - Simson Petrol
Wisp of Imagination - Stephen Hocking
Temporal Magic - Eric Rothermel
The Poem - Álvaro Serrano
Nature's Hand - Greg Shield
Head Over Heels - Alexander Godreau
Métro, Boulot, Dodo - Thor Alvis
The Tower Block - Pierre Châtel-Innocenti

Cover Image - Annie Spratt

Poetic Experiments is an ongoing series. For more, visit:

www.chrisgibsonart.com

www.ingramcontent.com/pod-product-compliance
Lightning Source LLC
Chambersburg PA
CBHW061300040426
42444CB00010B/2449